The Anointing Cost

Dr. Charmaine Bailey

Table of Contents

Dedication

This book is dedicated to Yeshua HaMashiach, Jesus Christ, with whom All things are possible, and with Him, I can do All things. Without Him, I can do nothing. Also, dedicated to my children and grandchildren, because of them, I fight the good fight, believing and praying by faith that they All will be saved and become True Men and Women of God, walking and working out their purpose in Christ our Lord and Savior. Jiwan, you may be with the Lord, but know that though you are gone physically, but you are with us spiritually and in our hearts always.

Acknowledgment

I acknowledge all of the Patriarch and Matriarchs of The Bailey Family, All of The Spiritual Leaders Who prophesied, prepared, taught, disciplined, prayed, and supported my ministry, nationally and internationally. I have to acknowledge those who meant bad, but Almighty God turned it for my good. Because at the end of it all, Romans 8:28 (KJV) says, “And we know that all things work together for good to them that love God, to them who are called according to His purpose.” To My Brothers and Sisters in Christ who are helping me on all the social media platforms, My Eagle Family, Upper room prayer experience—The Prophets Corner on YouTube, Instagram, and Facebook, I love you all to life. Peace, Love, and Blessings. You are Blessed to be a Blessing. God Bless You All!

About the Author

[Client will provide the information]

Page Left Blank Intentionally

Act One

The Family

Growing up in a large family as the firstborn of my mother's children and the first grandchild of my grandmother's grandchildren was surely a beneficial experience for me. My mother, may God rest her soul, was only 16 when she got pregnant with me. So, basically, I was raised by my grandmother, Odelia, but everyone called her Pat.

As a child, I used to live in a two-story old house. The house had a lot of character and spirit. I was brought up in a Christian Baptist family and church, and I was baptized at Ebenezer Baptist Church at the age of eight. I loved being in church, especially the praise and worship music. We were at church at least three times a week.

My great-grandmother, Rosanna Young, was the matriarch of the Bailey family. She stood 4'6" and was as sharp as a whip. She was a prophetess, a wise spiritual warrior, and a praying woman of God. I believe that's where my grandmother Pat received her intercessory prayer anointing. It was inherited.

I still remember my great-grandma Rose, who would come for Sunday dinner like clockwork at 4 p.m. every Sunday. She would have all the grandkids, and me lead the line, and we would have to quote scripture to her. As a reward, we would get two pennies, Tootsie Rolls, and peppermint candy. I loved it.

Even in school, I was an overachiever, staying on the honor roll in elementary and middle school. I was a dreamer and a writer who loved to write poems and poetry in elementary, middle, and high school as well.

Now, my mother, Saundra — she was a breed of her own. A dark-skinned woman, very mystical, spiritual, and a warrior both physically and spiritually. Even before she got pregnant with me, and while she was carrying me, my mother was in a girl gang that would go to different parts of the city. They would fight others, even the boys. Mind you, this was back in the mid-1960s.

I remember my great-grandmother telling me I was a special child and to never forget it, that God was going to use me. I was about five years old, sitting and watching TV. Then I left the room, came back, and told my mom and grandma:

"I'm going to grow up and be a great humanitarian."

They looked at each other with amazement and asked, "Where did you hear that word from?"

I hunched my shoulders and said, "I don't know, but that's what I'm going to be when I grow up."

I lived in a home with my grandma, granddad, my mom, my two aunts, one uncle, and three cousins. Then my mom had five more children — three sisters and two brothers — but she raised them all. I had a connection to my mom but a stronger connection to my grandma, who raised me in the truest sense.

My eldest aunt had one son, and my other aunt, who was my mom's sister and shared the same dad, had two sons. She was named after my grandma. My great-granddad was a very handsome man of fair complexion with light, grayish-colored eyes — a very spiritual man.

However, because he wasn't taught about his prophetic gift, his anointing was exploited by the leader of the church he attended. He would tell people things about themselves, and it would come to pass. He also did spells, thinking it was to help people, and the leader would get payment for his work.

But there was one woman who wanted my great-granddad to put a love spell on her daughter's boyfriend so he would marry her. The spell backfired, and the man ended up marrying another woman. That woman was so infuriated with my great-granddad that she put a spell on the woman in my great-granddad's family that they wouldn't marry or stay married.

The first person to marry one of my grandmother's children was my aunt. She was the baby girl of my grandma's children and was married for close to ten years. She had one daughter, then divorced, and hasn't married again. Now, she is almost 70 years old. None of my grandmother's children ever married, but the curse has been broken.

My great-granddad went home to be with the Lord in the mid-1970s. I remember it as clearly as if it were today. The ambulance came, and my great-granddad slept in the back room that I always stayed in as a child, sitting in front of his big box TV watching *Charlie Brown* or westerns. My great-granddad loved cowboy and western movies.

As the paramedics wheeled him out through the house, the living room door was opened, and the song playing on the radio was "Me & Mrs. Jones" by Billy Paul. At that time, the black urban radio station was named WAMO. I believe it stood for the three rivers that met at the point in Pittsburgh, PA. They are the Allegheny, Monongahela, and Ohio Rivers.

As my great-granddad entered the ambulance, I had a feeling he was coming back, but he didn't; he died at the hospital.

After his death, my great-grandmother remarried, and her husband passed away years later. My grandmother and I would go stay overnight with her on Saturdays. All of us would go to church together on Sundays and have Sunday dinner as a family. Those were the good old days.

My granddad, grandma, and I would take long rides to the country, go bowling, or visit family and friends on the weekends. It was just the three of us, and I believe that's where I grew my love for traveling, both nationally and internationally. Then, my great-grandmother went home to be with them in the late 1990s.

It was a large going-home celebration for her. At that time, it was just my grandmother and her two brothers left. My uncle would drive from West Virginia to visit for the weekend, and we would talk about the Bible and church and pray together in a big circle. It was awesome, and I really liked it.

Later, in 2010, my grandmother went home to be with the Lord. One of her brothers had passed before her, and one after.

As for my mom, I loved her, and we grew closer in her later years. At the time, I was living in Atlanta, GA, where I was ordained as a Pastor and an Elder on November 29, 2008. My mother took ill and asked me to come home to help her.

I said, "Mom, you have five other children."

She replied, "But I need you to come back and help me."

I then heard a voice within me say, *"Honor thy father and thy mother, so that thy days may be long upon the land which the Lord thy God giveth thee."*

I had been living in Georgia from 2007 until 2012, and then my three sons and I returned to our hometown.

Act Two

Teenage-Young Adulthood

At this time in my life, I felt different, like I didn't fit in. The loss of some of the most significant and influential family members was hard to bear. Their roles in my life left a huge impact on me and helped me stay grounded in my faith.

I loved being around older people because they knew so much. I would just listen to their stories, history, traditions, and faiths. As I entered my teenage years, I was surrounded by friends at school, but when I came home, it was a whole different story. We were a big family, still living in a two-story house, and I had a lot of "me time." During that time, I would write. Being a studious person, I always finished my homework at school.

My mom was always playing hiding games with us and even with other adults. We would walk into a room, and she would be standing behind a door, jumping out to scare the pants off us. She loved watching scary movies. We would pop popcorn and watch *Chilly Billy* every Saturday night at 11:30 p.m. after the late news.

My mom was a fighter, and I inherited that quality from her. I was a bit of a tomboy, climbing apple and peach trees, playing "Release the Dent," dodgeball, kickball, baseball, running track, and playing hide-and-seek. As I grew into my teenage years, there were more boys than girls on our street. One of the boys was the street bully, and he would hit me with a piece of rope from the clothesline. One day, he hit me so hard it left a welt on my arm, and boy, did it sting. Yes, I cried for a little while. When my mom asked me what happened, I was scared to tell her because she didn't play, but I told her the truth anyway.

And, boy, I saw steam come off her head. She said, "Get back out there and hit him back."

I hesitated, and she replied, "Let's go," holding an extension cord in her hand.

All the kids were outside playing, and I walked up to the big bully — who was fat, too! I hit him, and he punched me back. I looked at her. She said, "Either you beat him up, or I'm gonna beat you up."

I saw that extension cord and started throwing my hands everywhere. I got a couple of good hits in, and then the fight was over. She took me into the house and said, "You have to learn to fight back. If you don't, they will keep picking on you. You have to show them you're not scared of them."

The bully never messed with me again after that.

My mom would tell us things I didn't understand as a child, but as I got older, it made perfect sense. My mom was the life of the party. She had a beautiful dark complexion and dressed really nicely. But one thing she wouldn't do was hug or kiss us or tell her children that she loved us. I didn't understand it because my grandma and great-grandmother would, but not my mom.

When I started high school in ninth grade, I was ready. You couldn't tell me nothing. Now, this part of my life is where the older people would say, "You're smelling yourself." It's like you think you know it all, and now you don't want to listen to wise counsel.

But I had met a young guy. He played for the football team. Me? No sports in high school.

I started shying away from people. I had gone to the doctor, and I noticed patches of my hair falling out. The doctors diagnosed me with Alopecia. It's a disorder — a deficiency in the immune system where your hair follicles are attacked. I started getting homeschooled and would wear scarves on my head or a hat. I dealt with this for three years, on and off.

I started drinking beer and stealing my mom's Kool cigarettes. I noticed this was what the cool kids did, but my boyfriend didn't like it. He was a jock. Eventually, we broke up but remained friends.

I was 16 years old, going to the dances and kids' clubs. My friend and I would go together, and there would be these rivals at the parties, too. Every Friday and Saturday night, we would drink, dance, and then fight every time we saw each other. There were times they would try to jump me, but my friend — she wasn't a fighter — still, she would always run her mouth.

When I was 17 years old, I was coming from my friend's house. There were these three guys talking, and one guy said, "Where you going?"

I said, "Home."

I had missed my bus, so he offered to walk me home. But we started drinking and talking, and I didn't make it home. We stayed at his dad's house. The next day, he took me home, and we became friends. Then he was my boyfriend.

I didn't go to prom the following year because I was pregnant, and he went to jail right before I had our daughter.

I was mad at him but so glad that I had a little me to love and care for. I left school and went on to get my high school diploma a couple of years later. I got my own place in the projects — a one-bedroom apartment on the third floor. I hated walking up all those stairs. But it was all mine. Now, you really couldn't tell me nothing!

But even in this state — promiscuous, drinking, smoking — I started dating again because my daughter's father was in jail.

This man was older and a drug dealer. He gave me nice things and money. But I knew it wasn't right. Then, another man came into the picture. He would shower me with gifts and attention, but he was already married. I had just had my son about nine months ago, but we fooled around for a little over a year.

Then I moved across town. My sister and I became next-door neighbors; I am just one and a half years older than her.

It was the 1990s, and the crack epidemic was in full swing. Every state, every race, the poor and the rich, was addicted to this new drug called crack cocaine. I smoked it and sold it. I had a lot of connections, especially boyfriends, both new and old. That's how I met my third son's father — we would get high together.

I started noticing things that other people didn't see or hear. They would say, "Oh, you're crazy or paranoid," but it was a gift. As a child,

I would see things, hear things, and know things I couldn't possibly explain. I would tell others what I knew about them, even though I didn't know them from a can of paint.

It started coming back. I knew it was time to stop because of the fights and arguments with others, even with family members. So, I had three more sons while living in that addictive, promiscuous cycle, truly wanting a way out but not yet ready to stop partying. After six years, I finally moved back close to my family.

By 1996, I started going back to school and working. Everything was going well until I met a man who tried to take my life. This happened three times, but God's mercy and grace saved me every time. I was still covered by the prayers of my great-grandmother, great-grandfather, grandmother, and family.

I know they saw me as this predominantly young girl destined to do big things in life, but I was lost, hurt, and broken on the inside. Something was missing.

I had my baby girl in 1999, but she lived with her dad. There was a lot of manipulation and control in that relationship. We stayed in a family division, and I had two kids with him, including a son in 1992.

By 2001, I was living with my sister and began seeing things — dark figures, different smells — but for some reason, I wasn't scared at all. Remember, my mom raised me to be a fighter, a warrior physically. But now, I was seeing, hearing, and smelling things spiritual.

I moved into a three-bedroom house in a different neighborhood and started being around people I had met there. One of them was a gay man in a relationship, but he was my best friend. We did a lot together and experienced a lot.

There was another friend whose sons lost their mother under unclear circumstances. We would party together. She lived out of state and was in a gay relationship, but she identified as bisexual. I never judged. I just loved people.

"Be the best you can be and be true to thine own self!" That's my motto.

I remember one time my friend went on a beer run, and I had some pills. I took two of them, laid back on the couch, and started drifting away.

All of a sudden, I felt one of the hardest slaps on my face. I knew it wasn't a physical person.

I said, "What the heck?"

I called my friend, and he said, "I'm almost there."

No one else was home with me. I believe it was my angel. It wasn't my time to leave yet.

In 2004, I moved three streets over into another three-bedroom house. Around this time, my eldest daughter's dad, the one who went to jail when I was pregnant with our first child, got out of jail, and we started seeing each other again. He drank, and so did I.

I was still indulging in crack cocaine, though not like I had before. I was more of a drinker. My drink of choice was E&J with Pepsi on the rocks and a Budweiser beer. I'd go to the local bar — it was like Cheers, where everybody knows your name. That's where I'd be during happy hour and some weekends.

I could feel a turning point approaching in my life. One day, we were just sitting around talking, my daughter's dad and me.

"Well," he said, "all the kids are mine, no matter who their dads are."

Then he said the golden words my heart, soul, and spirit needed to hear: "Why don't you go to church?"

He added, "That church up the street is having a three-day revival."

I called my sister, who lived across from the church, and asked her if she'd like to go.

She said, "Yes."

That was August of 2005.

Act Three

Rededicating My Life Back To Yeshua Jesus!

My sister and I went to a three-day Prophetic Ministry Revival in August 2005. It was from Friday through Sunday. It was a spiritual awakening that felt like the experiences I had as a child in the Baptist Church, but this time, it was with a higher power, an energy or electrical surge, if I may say so. On the first day, I felt a connection to God — the God I always knew was there — but I couldn't get that kind of high anywhere else. Not from a drug, drink, sex, or money. This was what my soul had been crying out for.

I went back on the second day and again on the third day. On that third day, I went up for prayer and joined the ministry. When I got home, I told my child's father and asked him, "Will you be joining me and the kids? We need to all go as a family."

He said, "Maybe next Sunday," as he finished his beer.

So, the kids and I started attending every Sunday. Even my sister and her kids joined us. Eventually, my brother and his girlfriend also joined, along with some other family members. My mom, grandmother, two aunts, and a couple of my nieces and nephews started coming too. It became like a family affair.

It was so exciting when the Prophetess would lay hands on us and tell us what thus saith the Lord. Her words resonated with what was going on in my life, as well as some near-future events she foresaw.

There was also an Elder and a Deacon, both physically blind but spiritually sharp. Then there was an evangelist — there was something about her.

I had to keep praying because I couldn't quite put my finger on it, but eventually, I got my answer. About a month later, I asked my boyfriend the same question again, "Are you gonna be coming to church with us?"

His response was, "No, the church thing isn't for me, but you and the kids keep going." Then he added, "I see a change in you, Maine."

That's what he called me. My family called me Maine, but most friends or acquaintances called me Char.

I told him, "You've got to go. We're trying to live right now. No more smoking, drinking, or secular music. If you're not willing to even try to change, you have to leave. Go! Stay with your sister."

She lived about ten houses over the hill. He got mad, cussed, and tried to pick a fight. I turned on my Gospel music, and he left.

I said, "Lord! Thank you for taking the desire away from me. Anything that isn't right, take it away," and Yeshua Jesus did. I didn't need to go to NA (Narcotics Anonymous), AA (Alcoholics Anonymous), or SA (Sex Addicts Anonymous). My God took the self-gratification and all the things that my flesh and Satan wanted me to stay addicted to!

As time went on, I truly sold out for Christ and the Kingdom of God. I started meeting new like-minded church members. Then, I had a strange encounter. We fasted a lot in this ministry, and I remember one

Sunday morning during praise and worship, I started feeling very hot inside. Suddenly, I began speaking in a strange language.

The Pastor came to me and said, “Keep on speaking. Your tongues are coming.”

I kept going. I was speaking in an Indian language, or so the Pastor said. From then on, I kept fasting and praying for more of Him — Yeshua Jesus. I fell deeply in love with Him.

After that, my spiritual eyes were opened, and I began seeing and hearing more in the spiritual realm than ever before. One Sunday afternoon, just after getting home from church, I was in the basement washing clothes. I was singing a gospel song by Yolanda Adams, feeling joyful and happy in the Lord.

There was a divider wall in the basement. Suddenly, I felt a cold sensation on the back of my neck. As I turned, I saw a large black shadow — about thirteen feet tall or maybe even taller. Half of the figure was wrapped around the wall. I felt boldness, courage, and power rise up in me.

I spoke out, “You know you’re not supposed to be here. Satan! Get out, you and your demons!”

The black figure flew up the basement steps. I went back to singing and finished washing and drying the clothes.

Later, I called the Pastor and asked to set up a meeting about some things happening in my home. I was renting from an African woman named Mrs. Mbandi, who was going to school to become a minister.

She and I would periodically talk about the Lord. She was a nice landlady.

When I met with the Pastor, there was another Pastor there as well. I shared my experiences in the house — how I saw dark figures in the basement and the attic, where my sons slept. I noticed my sons becoming rebellious. I would discipline them, but the Pastors told me to keep fasting and praying. They gave me anointing oil and said, "Make a cross with it over your doors, windows, and bedrooms."

I asked, "Can't you come and anoint my house?"

They said, "No. You have to do it."

I was so upset with them. I prayed, "Holy Spirit, please help me get this demon out of the house."

On another occasion, I was in the living room, listening to Gospel music. I had two pieces of black leather furniture. Out of the corner of my left eye, I saw the figure of a large, fat physique man, but it was his spirit.

I said, "Who are you?" Then I added, "You need to go to the light."

The spirit disappeared. Later, I asked my neighbor who had lived in the house before me. She said, "A fat, obese man lived there with his wife and kids."

My boys continued to argue and fight upstairs in the attic. One day, I went up there and anointed both of them with oil. I prayed over them, and anointed their beds, shoes, doors, doorknobs, and windows. I wasn't playing. Whatever spirit or demon had them acting out like that — it was stopping.

"Enough is enough," I declared.

Now, there was a brother in Christ. He was my friend. We would go to church functions, watch Bible movies, and have discussions about them. If I needed to go anywhere, he was right there for me. One time, we were watching a movie in my home. The living room had panel boards on the walls. I looked out of my peripheral vision and saw a black spirit posted on the panel.

I asked my friend, "Do you see anything in here?"

To my surprise, he said, "Yes. I see that black figure on the panel to your right."

I said, "Yes, you see well."

We started praying, and it vanished. After the movie, he left.

***

A couple of days later, I was in the attic, battling this unclean spirit. My brother called and said, "I'm on my way. It's leaving today."

As I walked around upstairs, speaking in tongues and telling the demon it had to go, my kids opened the door for my brother. I told my kids to start praying, but my brother said, "Send them up to my sister's house."

Before I sent them, my brother said, "It's in the attic."

He ran up those stairs so fast that all you heard was heavy thumping. Then my brother shouted, "It's running down there!"

I saw a black spirit run into the basement. My brother was, and still is, a spiritual warrior, just as I am. When he ran into the basement, the light went out, and the kids started crying.

I told them, "You all can go now to your auntie's house."

Meanwhile, my brother and the dark spirit were in the hallway, tussling. My kids asked, "Who is he fighting with?"

With the physical eye, you could see my brother fighting the air. But with the spiritual eye, you could see him combating a dark entity, which was a demon. Then my brother said, "Open the front door!"

I did, and the spirit flew across the street into an abandoned building.

The kids ran up to my sister's house. My brother and I stood on the porch, jumping up and down, giving God the praise.

***

We went to church the following Sunday and gave our testimony. Boy, if looks could kill, the Pastor didn't like what I said. I told the Congregation that I had asked both pastors to come and do a spiritual cleansing in the home, but they both told me to take the anointing oil and do it myself. The Congregation was appalled. I noticed right then and there a change in the heart of the Pastor toward me. I was getting more and more elevated in the spirit.

Then, a new Man of God came to the church as an overseer. He was a Prophet of God. He would always talk with me about prophecy and how Yeshua Jesus was using me. He told me, "You are going to go higher into dimensions and to different countries."

I couldn't believe what he was telling me. But I had always been someone who traveled, going somewhere. When I was 12 years old, my aunt moved down south. I would speak to her on the phone, and she told me I was welcome to visit her anytime. Well, I saved up my money, got myself a Greyhound ticket, and went down south.

"Here I come!" I thought.

My grandma and family were looking for me all that day, calling friends and riding around. At 10 p.m., I called my aunt on a payphone and said, "You remember, you told me I can come and see you anytime?"

She said, "Yes."

I replied, "Well, I'm here."

She asked, "Where?"

I said, "I'm at the Greyhound bus stop."

She called the family back home, and they were relieved. My grandma and granddad came. I stayed for a week. It was hot, and the bugs were super big, but I enjoyed my stay.

***

Back in the present, while we were in home, my ex-boyfriend and my daughter's father — who I had broken up with — took one of the boys' keys when he picked them up from school. He got a copy made.

One night, at about 2:00 a.m., I heard the Lord say, "Go downstairs and lay on the couch."

So I did. As I lay down, I saw the doorknob turn. I asked, "What is it, Lord?" Then my kid's dad opened the door.

I jumped up and asked, "What are you doing here at this time of the morning?"

He had been drinking; I could smell it. He said, "I just want to talk to you."

I said, "No. Go."

He started coming toward me. I pushed him away. He lunged at me again. I picked up the lamp and hit him with it. As I struggled with him, he threw me to the ground. The only light on was the hallway light, beaming down on me as I lay on the ground with him over me, choking me.

I looked at him. His face was disfigured. I saw another face in his face. It was ugly — it was a demon. I had actually seen it. The demon tried to get him to kill me. But in an instant, I hollered, "Jesus!"

He let go of my neck. When he looked at me again, he was his true self. He started crying, saying, "Maine, I'm so sorry. Oh my God, oh my God, what did I do?"

Gasping for air, I said, "I forgive you. It wasn't you; it was a demon. I saw it. But you have to go and don't come back."

It was snowing outside, and all I could see were his footprints in the snow.

The next day, I got my locks changed.

As we went to The Pastor's Ordination, all that time, we were calling her Pastor, but she was actually an Evangelist. We would have her brothers and sisters in Christ come to the church periodically. For this Pastoral service, there was one in the morning and another in the evening, which was when The Pastor officially got ordained.

In the morning service, I had just read the announcement for the Pastoral Ordination Service. Then, two Prophetesses came from a neighboring church. They were prophesying about the ministry. One of the Prophetesses said that the ministry was the church of Sardis. I thought to myself, *Oh wow, that's not good,* for Sardis is one of the seven churches Yeshua Jesus speaks of in the Book of Revelation.

Then, the Prophets spoke and said, "Sister Charmaine, please come into the pulpit area."

Mind you, the Pastor and her sisters and brothers in Christ were all there. But when I got up to the pulpit, the Prophet said, "Now all the Prophets are in the house."

The only ones in the pulpit were the Prophet, the two Prophetesses from the neighboring church, and me. I was flabbergasted. My mom, grandma, and family members' mouths flew open. The Pastor had a look in her eyes as she gazed at me in the pulpit. She was sitting among the people of the Congregation.

Then a Caucasian woman stood, and the Prophet told me, "Lay your hands on her belly and speak what thus sayeth the Lord."

I did just that. As I laid my hands on her belly, I felt a bubbling up in my stomach, and words came flowing out of my mouth. The prophetic word was more so the Lord rebuking her and warning her, for she was a false prophet. Yeshua Jesus didn't give her the words she was speaking to people.

After that word, my hand started shaking immensely, and I fell to the ground. Then, the Prophet whispered in my ear, "This is your coming-out party."

He helped me up, and I had a prophetic word for the whole Congregation. The Pastor was full of jealousy toward me from that point on. So were her "flying monkeys" — those she manipulated, intimidated, and controlled.

I kept asking the Lord, "How much longer?"

He said, "Soon."

I went on a 21-day fast and asked the Lord, "Lord, the Prophet called me out and said I was a Prophetess. But Lord, who do you say I am?"

The Lord said, "My daughter, I have chosen you as my Prophet — not just any Prophet, but a great Prophet that I Am sending to the nations."

The whole house shook. We don't have earthquakes in my hometown, so I called my mom and the landlady because I was renting. A crack appeared above the basement door that wasn't there before. It was evidence that something had taken place in the home. But as the

Word of God says, when He comes, He comes with a shaking. Yes, it was a divine visitation.

I took a picture. The landlady knew because I would minister and prophesy to her.

Later, the church was having a retreat in the hills of West Virginia. The Pastor and some others invited me, so I went and bought some new clothes. My mom was at my home, and she was going to watch the kids for the weekend.

It was Friday morning when I got a call from the Pastor. She said, "I'm not going to be able to make it, but my Caucasian Prophetess sister in Christ will be picking you up."

I went upstairs to get dressed in my all-white outfit. The Lord said, "You are not going."

I said, "I'm not going?"

He said, "No."

As I put on my sandals and walked out of my bedroom, my brand-new skirt ripped from the top to the bottom. I said, "Wow, Lord. Okay, I guess I'm not going."

I called the Pastor and said, "I'm not going to be able to make it either."

And that was that. But they had something unsettling they were planning to do to me. God intervened, though!

After that, her true nature and character revealed themselves. A lot of people left the ministry. I saw a demon in the basement of her home, and so did a young man named Big Mike. (God rest his soul.) Her response to me was, "I like to keep my friends close and my enemies even closer."

I had a sickening feeling after she said that.

The Lord told me to write a letter to the church and to her. It was to be done decently and in order. It was my goodbye letter.

The only ones in that service were me, my mom, her, the Pastor, and the Evangelist. I usually sat in the back row, but I was led to sit in the front row. As she preached, she was calling me Judas. Her message was on Judas Iscariot from the Book of Matthew.

A dark spirit came toward me, but it couldn't touch me. I saw two angels in front of me. When the service ended, I went to hand her the letter. She wouldn't accept it, so I laid it on a chair.

My mom and I walked out, and as I opened the door, I said, "Thank God Almighty, I'm free at last. Thank God Almighty, I'm free at last."

I never went back there again.

Once, I saw her in passing, and she said to me, "Don't forget where you got your start from!"

I just laughed and said, "God bless you, Pastor."

That was the last time I saw her.

I called the landlady, Mrs. Mbandi, and told her what was going on in the house. I found a new home in another area, so she came to do the walk-through so I could get my security deposit back. She was hesitant to go into the basement.

I looked at her and said, "It's gone."

She smiled.

I told her, "You have no reason to be afraid. For it says in 2 Timothy 1:7, 'For God has not given us a spirit of fear, but of love, power, and a sound mind.' Amen."

Then we started attending a new church where we had moved to.

Act Four

The Ministry

As I moved to another area in my hometown, I started going to a new ministry. From the last ministry, I met a sister in Christ. She was a prophetess, and we attended the new ministry with our children along with us. Even my friend and brother in Christ would accompany me to this ministry at times as well.

It was a nice ministry, and I grew a lot there. They called me an Evangelist. I'm not one to be stuck in titles or positions, but I know what Yeshua Jesus spoke to me. As I attended this ministry, I became very spiritually awakened. I would always sit in the back of the church and watch.

I had asked God, "Why am I here?"

He told me, "To learn not to bring into the ministry I am birthing through you."

Once, I came in through the front door of the house of God and saw a black spirit fly past me and go down the steps. There was another time when people were all in line to be prayed over, and a woman was demonically possessed. The demon had her hollering, shaking immensely, and running around. They finally took her to the back rooms of the church. The elders were engaged in intense spiritual warfare.

Then, I finally got my day to preach. It was a prophetic word to the church, all scriptures. I don't believe they ever asked me to preach again. Some of my family members came to support me.

Another time, as people came up to be prayed for, I kept discerning this particular man. He was tall, about 6'2", and hefty — a few extra pounds. The Elderess and the Bishop of the church were the ones praying and laying hands on the people. But when this man stood before them, the Bishop prayed harder for him and started speaking in tongues.

As I looked in the spirit, I saw the Bishop pulling at the man's chest area. I saw a spirit, about a quarter of the way out of this man's chest, and he was laughing at the Bishop and the Elderess. The Elderess looked at me as if to say, "Help us!" But the Lord told me to be still and not go up there.

The man's laugh echoed through the whole church as I looked on, desperately wanting to help them. The Bishop struggled with that demon in the man. Then, all of a sudden, the Bishop and the Elderess fell to the ground. People from the Congregation went over to help them up.

The possessed man turned and walked away. As he left, he looked over at me. He didn't say a word but walked out of the church.

I asked the Lord, "Why couldn't they cast that demon out of that man?"

The Lord said, "Because of the sinful lifestyles they are living. Bishop is an angry man, always belittling his wife in front of the Congregation. He drinks strong drinks and smokes cigarettes. The

Elderess is in a homosexual relationship. I do not dwell in an unholy temple. There are people who have a form of godliness but deny the power thereof, which is the power (Dunamis) of the Holy Spirit."

I was stunned and said, "Wow, Lord."

Again, He said, "Just be still and know that I Am God. These are things you are not to bring into the ministry I Am birthing through you."

The following Sunday, the Bishop called me into his office. We discussed some things taking place in the ministry. My sister in Christ — I was often with her — was called Jezebel by the Bishop. They would both laugh about it. I didn't find it funny.

Even in the last ministry I attended, she came at the end of the year. She left before me. Both the Pastor and the Prophet warned me about her and told me to be careful, but they never said why. I did see some manipulative behavior and control issues with her. Yes, those are indicators of a Jezebel spirit. She introduced me to the Pastor of the next church home I would join.

As the Bishop and I were speaking, I asked him, "Who in this ministry has a deliverance ministry or calling? That's what needs to be done here — a true deliverance service starting with leadership and going all the way through."

He didn't respond. I understood why. A deliverance service would include him needing to be delivered as well.

About a month later, the Lord told me to write my letter to the church and Bishop. It was time to move on.

So, the prophetess, my three boys, her husband, and I started attending a new ministry. It was held in a hotel conference room. I got to know the Pastor very well. She became my spiritual mother in the Lord. She was an older saint, but she was very wise and humble. Her mother was a part of her ministry. She ordained me in 2007 as an Evangelist but later started calling me Prophetess.

My friend, the man who attended certain churches with me, also came to this ministry. There was a prophetess in the house, and she prophesied that my friend and brother in Christ was my kingdom husband. We both laughed and said, “No!” every time she spoke those words.

I praise God for the support of the Bishop, his wife, and some of the leaders of his Congregation. When Pastor ordained me as an Evangelist, they showed up — my mom, grandma, a couple of family members, and my friend and brother in Christ, David.

I had 7 plaques made and handed them to each person who impacted my life up to that point in my spiritual walk. Each plaque had words engraved on it about what they meant to me. It was so beautiful. Pastor also had a theological school that I attended for four years. Through her school and teaching, I received my Bachelor’s, Master’s degree, and a Doctorate in Divinity. She also had sons in ministry.

Now, my sister in Christ was married to an African man, and there was another African man who joined the ministry. Pastor tried to set me up with this man. I knew something wasn’t right about him — he was hiding something. But I told her, “No, thank you. Pastor, that man is married, and his wife and kids are living in Africa.”

She tried to convince me that wasn't true. So, she set that man up with her goddaughter. The goddaughter had two sons, one of whom was autistic, but he just needed to be delivered. There was a demon possessing him.

I was blessed with the gifts of healing and deliverance.

It was February 2007, one of the coldest and snowiest storms my hometown had ever experienced, and that day, I was moving. The Lord told me, "It's time to move." I got that U-Haul truck, packed my things in it, and my niece and her husband drove their car. I was in Georgia the next day. I had fasted and prayed for the Lord to move me. I love to travel anyway, so I was ready to go!

Act Five

It's February 2007, and now my sons and I are living in Marietta, GA, in a beautiful complex. We had a gazebo, and I started having Saturday morning believers' service at 10:00 a.m. I would teach and preach the word of God to a handful of people. Then, as the people started multiplying, we moved the service from the gazebo to "Service of the Lake," where I would feed the people spiritually and then feed them physically. There were small BBQ pits built in the ground, and a lake ran through the apartment complex.

I noticed one Saturday morning that a beautiful white and pink swan swam up and posted right there where we were. The swan was actually listening to the message, and every Saturday we were there, that same swan was there. There, I learned so much about being a spiritual leader — being humble, fasting, and praying like never before, seeking Yeshua Hamashiac (Jesus) more. I was being elevated spiritually.

We have to understand that life is truly spiritual. You are a spiritual being first and foremost, as the word of God says, "To be absent from the body is to be present with the Lord." That's your spirit man being connected to God. You have a physical body that is going back to the dust. From the dust, you were made, and to dust, you shall return. And you have a soul, your mind, which is the alive, conscious part of you.

I was having many dreams from God, and the Spirit of the Lord was placing songs in my heart. As I wrote every song down, I would hear actual music, like the beat or melody to the song.

A couple of months later, some family members came to visit. We had a service in the morning, and that evening, we sat around talking about those who had gone home to be with the Lord and those who were doing well or bad in our family. My two sons went to the store. It was a large two-lane road they had to cross to get to the store. What really happened was my youngest son was following his older brother, and as my older son ran across the street, his younger brother ran behind him and got hit by a moving car.

My daughter's father was coming down the road. He saw the police and ambulance and asked what happened. When he saw it was my son, he came down the hill and got me. The other family members and friends who were there, some drove up to the little highway. I ran up there. They had put my son in the ambulance. The driver of the car who hit my son said, "It happened so fast, I didn't see him." The man was crying.

My son said he turned around as he got to the other side of the road. He heard a loud noise and a car screeching. My son flew up in the air and fell to the ground.

When we got to the hospital, the doctors said it was a miracle. They got a statement from the driver, who said he hit my son. The driver described how my son went up in the air, fell on the car, and then hit the ground. Only by the grace and mercy of God did my son have only a few abrasions, no head injuries, and no broken bones. Yes, Glory be to God! Nothing missing, nothing broken! He was released, but he was only 9 at the time. No charges were filed. It was an accident, and he wasn't hurt. All those prayers and fasting were paying off. I tell you, it's the anointing that costs.

As I stated in my prior chapter, while living in that apartment complex, I was growing more spiritually and gaining more understanding. I was elevated in my anointing and the gift of discernment. I was testing the spirit of everyone, even the animals.

This is where Apostle called me and said Almighty God spoke to him and said I was ready to be ordained. Before his call, two weeks prior, the Lord spoke to me and said, "My daughter, will you feed my sheep?"

I was like, "Huh? Feed your sheep, Lord? I'm already evangelizing and prophesying your word to your people." Then the Lord's voice got very firm but precise, in a loving way, and He said again, "My daughter, will you feed my sheep?"

With tears in my eyes, I said, "Yes, Lord, I will feed your sheep." Then I said, "Lord, that's a pastoral calling... okay, yes, Lord." Then, I started giving Yeshua Hamashiac (Jesus) the praise.

Two weeks later, that's when Apostle called, and I said yes. I gave him the date that came to my heart, which was November 29, 2008. Yeshua (Jesus) moved me from Marietta, GA, to Atlanta. Within six months, I was living in a ranch-style house — it was beautiful.

Then, I got my sons situated, enrolled them in school while I was visiting other ministries, and meeting new church leaders. Around August 2008, there were people I knew from my hometown living in Atlanta, GA, and one of their friends, a minister, was introduced to me.

The Lord directed me to go to a hardwood store, and he gave me the measurements for the wood, the color of the plywood, the paint, and the size of the nails we were to use to make our podium for the pulpit.

I said to the minister and my three sons, "I have to anoint your hands with anointing oil, for this is sacred; this is a holy object going into a holy place — the House of God."

As I anointed my sons' hands, it was such a blessing to watch them. Then I went to anoint the minister's hands, and he screamed, "It's burning! My hands are burning!"

My sons looked at him with confusion. I told them, "Go to your rooms." I told that minister, "You have a demon in you; that's why the anointing oil burned your flesh." I also told him he could not help put the podium together. I told him he needed to be delivered, and he needed to speak with his Apostle. If the Apostle didn't deliver him, I would do it by the dunamis power of the Holy Spirit in the name of Jesus.

Act Six

Ministry is in full swing in Atlanta, Georgia, and it was a good time for me. However, I noticed my sons were meeting new boys who seemed to be leading them astray.

I always advised my kids, "Before you call them your friend, discern the spirit in them. Do they help you or hinder you? Are they truly meant for you? Are they leading you in the right direction or taking you down a path to get in trouble in school, with the police, or anyone in Authority over you?"

So, I told them, "I want to meet all your friends."

I had two sons: one was in middle school, and the other just started high school. To my surprise, I found out that the vice principal at the middle school—my son attended—was my elementary school gym teacher. What a small world!

Both of my sons were very observant. They never got in trouble. Although, there were some minor school suspensions and detentions, nothing really major.

With that being said, my son, who was starting high school (ninth grade, to be exact), met up with the wrong two boys. Once, he was found in an abandoned building, cutting school. Later, in a stolen car—although he didn't steal it., he was guilty by association.

The series of incidents didn't stop there. Next came another incident—vandalism—and it was always with the same boy. Last time, he was sent to a detention center for 60-90 days, and that was the last time he got in trouble.

I had stopped my son from being with one of those boys. Afterward, I met his other friend's mom and came to the conclusion that they should not be hanging around each other anymore. Luckily, his mother moved to another area in Atlanta. Glory be To God!

***

The ministry was growing day by day. I was enjoying a good support system—two Prophetess, an Evangelist, and my son in the Lord, a Minister. It was a Prophetic Ministry and helped me specialize my gifts of deliverance and healing more so in this region.

There, I witnessed an amazing move of God. I remember meeting a Pastor once. She had a ministry close to my son's middle school, so I would see her from time to time. When my son in the Lord invited her to the church service, I learned that she and her male companion were not married. But, in the spirit, I saw that they were connected sexually and physically.

It was that time when we were in service, and I heard the Lord say, "It's gonna be a deliverance service today."

As we were calling people up for prayer, I saw a homeless man. He was the same man to whom I would give a plate of food and invite him to service. Finally, that day, he made his way there. So, he hollered out, "I don't know why, but I was led to come here today."

All I could say is *Thank You, Jesus.* It's been months trying to get him to come.

As I started praying over each person who came forward, the unclean spirit in him began to manifest. So, when it was his turn, he started convulsing and foaming.

I told them, "Get the kids. Anyone who is not filled with the Holy Spirit or does not want to take part in this deliverance, you may leave now. But, you, all the leaders and clergy, start praying and place your hands on this man."

He started speaking vulgarly as he was laid out on the floor. I knelt down on the floor with him, praying over him. I was quoting Scripture, telling the unclean spirit that its time is up. I said, "You can no longer take possession and control of this body."

I called out every unclean spirit in this man, "Vagabond, poverty, polluted alcoholism, drug addiction, bondage, and whoredom spirits, loose him now, in the name of Jesus!"

In the spirit, I saw three dark figures (demons) shoot out of his body. He was coughing immensely, bringing up large, smelly white phlegm, and it had a foul smell to it.

However, I kept praying over him. I said, "You are not getting up until you are filled with the Holy Spirit."

We know that it is speaking in tongues that tells us when we are filled with the Holy Spirit, according to Acts 2 - Acts 8. Anyway, he was delivered successfully.

Meanwhile, I saw that woman Pastor and her male companion run out the door in the middle of the deliverance! That tells you who is Holy Spirit Filled—a spiritual warrior for the kingdom of God.

Two weeks later, I, with my spiritual son, who is the minister, went to visit her ministry. When we got there, she and the Congregation had on army fatigues clothing. My spiritual son and I looked at each other like, "Wow! Just two weeks ago in my ministry, you and your male companion ran while deliverance was going on."

As A Prophet of Almighty God, I had a prophetic word for her and that ministry. Consequently, the word of the Lord convicted her heart, and she received a warning about the adulterous affair—she was having with her male companion.

She needed to be delivered as I spoke the word of the Lord to them. The Pastor went to her office and didn't return. That was the end of the service. Six months later, her ministry was shut down, and she went back to Florida.

Another deliverance was of a childhood-aged son. He was growling and acting out. His mother sent him to me to have me pray over him because she had no idea what was happening to her son.

As soon as I put the Anointing oil on his forehead—the frontal lobe is the forehead area, and the optic lobe is the back of the neck—he screamed and said, "It burns."

He was trying to wipe it off. However, as I laid my hands on him, he went out in the spirit. I spoke to that rebellious, manipulating, and argumentative spirit (witchcraft) that it was attached to the boy and rooted in his family. I mentioned that his grandad was a voodoo priest, so that demon was passed down through the genealogy lineage. Through the power of prayer, he was finally delivered. His mom said that she had seen a big improvement in her son. We gave Yeshua (Jesus) the Glory for that.

On another occasion, a woman came to my home and said, "Something is wrong with me." I knew right away what it was. So, I told her, "Come on in; I was expecting you."

My boys were away for the weekend. So it was great timing. The woman came on Friday evening, around 5-6 pm. We prayed, and she stayed overnight. The battle started that Saturday morning.

I was already reading the Bible and praying when she entered the room. I saw the spirit of witchcraft all over her. So, I put on some Worship music and told her to sit down at the dining room table. We both started reading the Bible.

It was the moment when she just had this glaze, frozen expression stuck on her face. I said, "You alright?"

She laughed and spoke, but it wasn't her voice; it was a deep voice speaking through her vocal cords.

I said, "That's it, it manifested."

She got up, and I stood up with her and touched her forehead. She went down as I caught her and laid her on the ground. I started speaking to that witchcraft spirit. No doubt, it was deep-rooted because she was practicing witchcraft and didn't even know the extent of it.

I told that spirit, "I break you off her bloodline."

It stopped. Then, I found that witch in her family's genealogical lineage. We had to go back to her great-grandfather (maternal) and her great-grandmother (paternal). Both sides of the family had dabbled and were performing witchcraft on others.

She was lying there, vomiting up a dark liquid, and the smell was horrendous—worse than when her hocker was white. Then, she started speaking in tongues. It was after 7 pm Saturday when she got her deliverance. I told her, "Go. Look in my living room mirror."

Her whole countenance changed. Her voice was back to her light-toned speaking voice. But the kicker was that she had changed three shades lighter. Her complexion was no longer that of a dark-skinned woman but of a brown-skinned woman. We put on Praise music and Glorified the Lord for about two hours, and then she went home. Delivered, saved, and set free. Amen.

Act Seven

It's 2012. I moved back to a city I didn't want to return to and told myself I wouldn't!

If you want to make God laugh, tell Him your plans because he has already made our plan.

According to Jeremiah 29:11: "For I know the plans I have for you, declares the Lord, plans to prosper you and not to harm you; plans to give you a hope and a future."

We were holding Sabbath (Saturday) church services in a building that houses Senior Citizens. The Social Worker allowed our ministry to come in and lead the Elders or Senior Citizens to the Lord.

I remember our first day there, how they came peeking in, wondering, *what is this that some of our elder brothers and sisters in the Lord were saying as they walked pass the room?*

We had a five-fold Prophetic Ministry. We believe in the Father (YAH), Son (Yeshua HaMashiac/Jesus the Messiah), and the Holy Spirit (Ruach HaKodesh).

We also portrayed the 9 gifts and fruits of The Holy Spirit. The Deliverance and Healing Ministry was also in full effect, demonstrated through the gifts the Holy Spirit has embodied me with and in the ministry at different times to help God's people, lost as well as saved.

There was an older woman who came to me and said, “I have been praying to Jesus to bring a Sabbath Ministry to us, and look, he sent you. God does answer prayer.”

I said, “Yes, He does.”

I was directed by The Holy Spirit to hold church services on Saturdays, the Seventh Day of the week as it is written in the 10 Commandments Exodus 20:8-11: “Remember The Sabbath Day and keep it holy.” …. And that’s what I have been doing since 2007.

As I, by the unction of The Holy Spirit, was led to teach and preach, also prophesy over the Sabbath day ministry, leading them in Holiness and to Worship, Praise, and Glorify The Lord.

They learned to hear God’s voice, for the word of God says, “My sheep know My voice, and a stranger’s voice they will not follow.”

We have to learn to differentiate between God’s voice, Satan’s voice, and our own voice. Just be still and know that I am God! Just be still and hear that still, peaceful, soothing voice that comforts your spirit man.

Now, there was another ministry there that operated on Sunday morning. I started to notice snickering, belittling, gossiping, and jealousy from that ministry’s Congregation. One of the members of the ministry was related to the overseer of that ministry. So, I asked to have a sit-down with her to talk about some of the shenanigans going on with her members.

As I spoke to her, I saw where they got it from.

I said, "We are all God's children and when he made one ministry he didn't stop. We are the church and as his beloved children, we should be coming together in unity and one accord. God is not pleased with this. Now, we know you've been there for a while, but this is not about competition, for I am a humble woman of God. It is about my Father's business—guiding the souls and hearts of his people, lost as well as saved, back to Him and not to a man or woman who is supposed to be a servant, ambassador, and leader for Christ Jesus."

But there was a spirit, deep-rooted, and it was Jezebel. There was a controlling, prideful, but subtle spirit that was operating through her. I know that spirit very well and I spiritually fight against it on a constant basis. I hate evil and despise wickedness. These spirits (demons) hate us because we, human beings, were made in His likeness and in His image.

Satan is trying to gather all the souls he can to take to hell with him and his demons. So, there was continuous opposition from that ministry against my ministry because Jezebel hates the True Prophets of God! And I speak by the Authority of Yeshua Himself as a Prophet of God and His mouthpiece to the nations.

I truly believe that every ministry and denomination should have a deliverance service every month, prayerful that the spiritual leader has the gift of discernment, which tells the truth or error in a person, especially those of that Congregation.

I see why God brought me there. It was a spiritual battle, warfare for that territory—I see some of the older saints who were calling themselves Christians were living lukewarm lives.

We have to understand that when we get Saved, Baptized, and Filled with the Holy Spirit, there is a change, a transformation that takes place within us. You have picked up your cross and are now following His ways, will, and His word to the best of your ability. For, you are now a changed person. You are the light of the world, shining so brightly that people can see your light from miles away. You are the salt of the Earth, and they all want to taste that salt because it seasons every part of their being.

See Saints, My Anointing comes with a cost! You never know what someone has been through, going through for the sake of Christ—The Anointed One. So, for myself, everything I had to go through in life was exercising my Anointing, making it more strong each time I had to go through a spiritual fight and got the victory because of who I am in Yeshua (Jesus).

At the age of 13, raped by a childhood friend's stepdad, I was shamed, reproached, and rejected by peers because of an immune disorder called Alopecia. Then had backslidden, drinking and smoking to cover up the brokenness of my heart. Being shunned and getting no support from your own family members.

Having children out of wedlock, being in two abusive relationships, having a child die a teenager, feeling and knowing that people you know and don't know are so jealous of the anointing that they're doing witchcraft on me, paying mediums and psychics to monitor me. Trying to do exchanges and transfers in the spiritual realm to take my vision, virtues, Glory, purpose, star, and life, but they can't have it. God gave it, and only Almighty God can take it away.

I'm not leaving, even a crack opened, door, gateway, avenue, or portal for any witch or demon to come in, not with The Holy Spirit Power (Dunamis) that was given to me, nope, not a chance. I truly love the Lord Yeshua HaMashiac, The Christ, with all my soul, heart, mind, and strength. Nothing and no one comes before Him in my life, and I mean no one or nothing.

I love my angels who direct, minister and protect me and all those I pray and intercede for on a daily basis. In the ministry, I was led to feed the people spiritual food (the word of God/ the message) and then feed them physically with physical food (I would cook every Friday night and bring food into the service every Saturday morning, and we ate good chicken, salad, potato, rice, spaghetti, rolls, pizza, etc.). We had fundraisers, and we sold rib, chicken, or fish dinners every season.

Moreover, we had the children's ministry. We took the kids to an amusement park every summer with food and drinks for free.

I would also have a "Holy Ghost Party" for my birthday, more so on the Sabbath Saturday of my birthday. We would rent a large park ground every year and would have a DJ who played gospel music or line dancing music that both the old and young could enjoy.

We would also invite two other spiritual leaders, and then I would give each of us the same scripture. We had 20 minutes to preach or teach. In it, each one of us and you could see and hear how the Holy Spirit moved in each of us but with a different message but with the same scripture.

We had all the food you could eat, beverages, face painting, and balloon twisting for the kids, and after the messages to the people were over, we called them up for prayer, discipleship, and prayer of salvation.

There was a swimming pool right across from our meeting. If the person was ready to be baptized, we dunked them in a pool, said the baptism prayer over them, and invited them into the family of Christ Jesus, the Church. And All were— and are —welcome. I did it for 10 years.

I believe it truly stopped when the pandemic started. The building was shut down due to the Covid-19 pandemic. I was around senior citizens; some were dying a lot, and some were sick, so, yes, it was 2019 when our ministry ended with them in my hometown. And I moved on to another state and a new assignment.

Act Eight

The Lost Souls—Las Vegas, Nevada— a big, bustling city with breathtaking tourist attractions, lots of people, and hot weather. Some days were so hot it looked like an oasis. It is a desert with mountains and palm trees that bent at a 90-degree angle when the Santa Ana winds blew our way—wind storms, like how some states would have snow storms.

With a heart full of love, I liked being close to my daughter and three grandkids while the other grandkids were back in Pennsylvania. While I was living there, my first book was published, "*Inspirational Poems For Every Occasion,*" written by Dr. Charmaine Bailey. Not long after, I started an online channel on a social media platform, YouTube: *Upperroomprayerexperience—Host Dr. Charmaine Bailey*— every Saturday Sabbath at 11:00 AM PST.

As my subscribers grew, I found myself attracting different social media influencers and interviewers who did book interviews with me. So, one out of the four that stood out was the book interview on iHeartRadio with a man named Toby.

However, I must say that living in Vegas was a whole different experience and atmosphere for me. I understand why they call it "*The City of Sin.*" There are casinos and little gambling places on every other corner, really. The prostitution is very in-your-face, so to speak, not hidden, especially when these young women shared their stories with me—often dependent on a man and the drugs he supplies and a roof over their heads.

They really feel that these men who have manipulated and brainwashed them actually care for and love them. But as I would share with them, the love they should be looking for is the love of Christ, Yeshua (Jesus)!

The Scripture I would start off with is John 3:16: "For God so loved the world, that He gave His only begotten Son, that whoever believes in Him shall not perish but will have everlasting life." That tells them that God loves them so much that he sent his son, Yeshua (Jesus), here on Earth in a human form to save them.

And also, 1 John 1:9: "As we repent of our sins, He is faithful and just to forgive us our sins and to cleanse us from all unrighteousness."

That scripture lets them know that no matter what they have done, did, or will do; He will forgive them as long as they repent and truly mean it from the heart. Just ask Him to forgive us of every sin, iniquity, trespass, and transgression we have ever committed.

We just have to believe that He is Yeshua HaMashiach, The Christ Jesus! And we have to forgive others as well. I truly believe that the heart that Yeshua gave me is such that I would pick up and carry other's burdens and feel their pain, heartache, sorrow, and even their anger.

I feel that these women and people I spoke to, evangelized to, and prayed with were a part of my ministry. But what really got me was when I would prophesy to people who didn't know me from a can of paint. The amazement and excitement they had on their faces when I spoke the word of God confirmed what was in the secret places of their hearts.

As I stated before, I started a YouTube channel. My son was my tech man, for he went to college and graduated with an associate degree in videography media design. Now we have a second channel on YouTube: *Upperroomprayerexperience—The Prophets Corner.* This is a spin-off of a community-based television show I had in my hometown, which aired on PCTV-21 every week. Afterward, "The Prophets Corner" only stayed on for a year, 2006-2007. That was on assignment in Georgia.

Act Nine

On Assignment in Africa

I subscribed to a social media platform where I met people from all over the world— Australia, England, and even Africa. Those Brothers and Sisters I grew very fond of were from Ghana. I had built a ministry relationship with a couple of pastors and had an unforgettable experience in 2021 when I was invited to preach in Sunyani, Ghana. It was a 3-day prophetic conference, September 18-20, 2021.

I preached the first night; it was a Friday night that went smoothly because I usually hold services or meetings on the Sabbath Day, as I was instructed by The Lord years ago, as He did according to Luke 4:16 and throughout the New Testament.

So, the night was the first part of the day. Yes, it was a powerful message all about my best friend, "The Holy Spirit." The Congregation was on their feet, shouting and glorifying God. The anointing was so high there that I could feel the thickness in the atmosphere.

After the service, I prayed and prophesied over some of the church members, then went back to my hotel room. The next day, during our Saturday meeting, it rained so hard that even the lights went out for a while. However, Sunday service was more electrifying.

The Pastor preached an awesome word, and then he said to me, "Does the Prophetess have a word for the church?"

I said, "Yes, there is a word."

As I stood up to bring forth the word of the Lord to His people, I saw two unclean spirits in two of the young African men who were there. Suddenly, one man started to shake uncontrollably. I instantly knew it was a demon who was manifesting through him.

I said, "You, young man, come to the front."

Just as he came to the pulpit area, I told him what I had seen and why it came upon him. Hearing that, he repented of his sins. When I held out my hand toward him and started praying, he fell to the ground. However, I continued praying in tongues over him. He was convulsing and crying out to Yeshua (Jesus). Within a few moments, the unclean spirit left his body.

I needed him to speak in tongues —not an African tongue, but a tongue that he had never spoken before, signaling that the Holy Spirit was directing his speech and manifesting through him now. Finally, he was delivered and set free. Not long after, the other young African man who had been in bondage was also loosened from the unclean spirit. So, it turned into a deliverance service. However, on the other side, it was a blessing to see these people set free and Glorifying God!

Later, I met a WOG who was an administrator for Health and Drug Administration. She was beautiful. She, along with The Pastor and some of the church members, showed me around on a tour of Sunyani, Bolgatanga, Tamale, Kissimmee, and Accra, Ghana.

I was there for about two weeks, give or take a day. It was so beautiful there. I believe everybody should visit their motherland at least once in their lifetime.

Then, in 2022, I had the opportunity to visit Nigeria. It was a great life experience, too. There, I visited an Apostolic church as well. Although I was a bit under the weather, you still have to be prepared, in season and out of season.

There was a Prophetic word for the Congregation as well as a direct and individual word to the newly installed Pastor. She was married for over 20 years, and her husband, who was the Bishop, went on home to be with the Lord. *To be absent from the body is to be at one with the Lord.*

Two weeks prior to my arrival in Nigeria, The Pastor was in a terrible car accident. Her car was totaled, but The Lord spared her life. She received The Prophetic word from the Lord. The Lord spoke about her receiving a new car, as well as a better building house of God, new spiritual children coming, and the majority of the world being of the Prophetic Calling.

Indeed, God works in mysterious ways. He may not be there when you want Him, but He will be there right on time. He is an on-time God. Yes, He is.

Later, I met a family there. They showed me African hospitality and different foods and places that we visited. I enjoyed myself there, too!

So, Saints, God is not done with me yet. Yeshua HaMashiach said that my latter days shall be greater than my former, and so it shall be. It's now the year 2025. What a blessing to be among the land of the living, following the unction, direction, and instructions of The Holy Spirit, glorifying Yeshua HaMashiach, Jesus The Christ, with every fiber of my being, every gift—writing, singing, cooking, preaching, prophesying, edifying, exhorting, inspiring, and motivating His people both the lost as well as saved. Oh! Taste and see the goodness of The Lord.

In this year, 2025, the children of God and The Church Spirit man will come alive. I see spiritual growth like never before. The very ones whom people and society have frowned upon and turned a blind eye to are gonna be the very ones that Yeshua is gonna raise up for such a time as this! Because we are all God's children, created to be Holy, Righteous, and of The Divine Nature of our Creator. To the Saved and The Lost, it's The Anointed That Cost.

As I used different social media platforms, I met so many interesting Anointed Brothers and Sisters in Christ. In the meantime, I connected to a Ghanian Pastor who had invited me to preach at his three-day conference.

I told him, "I will pray about it and get back to you."

The Lord said, "Yes."

The need was fulfilled for me to go.

It was September 16, 2021, and an experience I will never forget. The greeting was awesome, considering how the younger woman was so humbled and carried everything for me. They treated me like a Queen. May she be treated with respect and honor with royal treatment.

I was amazed by the experience. The church conference was held in the city of Sunyani at a very prestigious hotel. I preached on the first day of the conference. My message was on "The Holy Spirit" and boy did He (the Holy Spirit) move in that place! It was a blessed time in the Lord.

The food was good. They knew I was a foreigner when I asked for a fork and spoon, as they typically eat everything with their hands there. So, it took some time for me to get used to it.

On the last day of the conference, which was on a Sunday, I was called up again.

The Pastor asked me, "Is there a word for the people?"

As I was in my office of A Prophet of God, I said, "Yes. There is a word for the Congregation."

Unbeknownst to me, that word turned the atmosphere into a place where I began to see demons manifest in a couple of the people there. Yeshua used me in the deliverance ministry to help two young African men. Both were shaking, almost convulsing, but I knew what was going on.

"You're coming out of them today!" I spoke to the unclean spirit in the first young man.

He kept turning away, but I would have him look at my face, in my eyes, so that the unclean spirit could see and feel the Dunamis Power of The Holy Spirit. I asked the young man a question or two that was relevant to the spirit I was dealing with, which was witchcraft. I knew someone had put a spell on him, and that spirit was angry, not wanting to leave the young man's body. It was comfortable as if the spirit had made its home there.

As the Congregation continued praying, I told it to come out. Within a few seconds, the man fell to the floor. They caught him and laid him down. He changed right before our very eyes. We kept praying and he started speaking in tongues, not in any African language either. We gave Yeshua Jesus the Praise after both men were delivered.

There was an older African woman who had a bad leg; she couldn't walk on it. So, she asked the Pastor if I would pray for her, and yes, I certainly did. As I did, something shot out of her leg (spiritually). She jumped up on the very leg and started crying, raising her hands up to give Yeshua (Jesus) Praise. In short, it was an incredible 3-day Prophetic conference meeting.

As we traveled, they showed me their beautiful country. I visited Accra, the capital of Ghana, then Sunyani city, where this 3-day conference was held. After that, we visited Bogatonga, where I stayed for a week, then traveled to Kissimmee and Tamale. I had a wonderful two-day stay in Ghana, Africa, and was treated like royalty.

Now, I see clearly that everything I had to go through in life was leading me to my destiny. My purpose in this life is to go to the hurt, broken-hearted, the poor, and those whom society and the world have turned their backs on.

I am called to speak the word of the Lord to His people— words of edification, exhortation, word of comfort, word of correction, and warning. I am here to give to those who are least fortunate, to stand for justice, and to live in Righteousness, Holiness, and the Divine nature of our creator. We must lead by example, for you will know them by their fruit. This is why The Anointing cost!

Glory Be To Yeshua HaMashiach! Love you All To Life! Forgiveness, Faith, Love, and Blessings Always. Shalom.

Made in the USA
Columbia, SC
28 May 2025

58535975R00037